# Dr. Seuss' ABC

HarperCollins *Children's Books*

57 59 60 58


ISBN: 978-0-00-715848-5


© 1963, 1991 by Dr. Seuss Enterprises, L.P.
All Rights Reserved
A Beginner Book published by arrangement with
Random House Inc., New York, USA
First published in the UK 1964
This edition published in the UK 2003 by
HarperCollins*Children's Books,*
a division of HarperCollins*Publishers* Ltd
1 London Bridge Street
London SE1 9GF

Visit our website at:
www.harpercollins.co.uk

Printed and bound in Hong Kong

# BIG A

little a

What begins with A?

Aunt Annie's alligator . . .

. . . . . A . . a . . A

# BIG B

little b

# What begins with B?

Barber
baby
bubbles
and a
bumblebee.

# BIG C

little          c

What begins with C?

Camel on the ceiling
C . . . . c . . . . C

# BIG D

little         d

David Donald Doo
dreamed
a dozen doughnuts
and
a duck-dog, too.

# ABCDE..e..e

ear

egg

elephant

e

e

E

# BIG F

## little          f

F .. f .. F

Four fluffy feathers
on a
Fiffer-feffer-feff.

# ABCD
# EFG

Goat
girl
googoo goggles
G . . . g . . . G

# BIG H

little            h

Hungry horse.
Hay.

Hen in a hat.
Hooray !
Hooray !

# BIG I

little        i

i . . . . i . . . . i

Icabod
is
itchy.

So am I.

# BIG J

little                    j

What begins with j?

Jerry Jordan's
jelly jar
and jam
begin that way.

# BIG K

little        k

## Kitten. Kangaroo.

Kick a kettle.
Kite
and a
king's kerchoo.

# BIG L
## little          l

Little Lola Lopp.
Left leg.
Lazy lion
licks a lollipop.

# BIG M

little            m

Many mumbling mice
are making
midnight music
in the moonlight . . .

mighty nice

# BIG N

little n

What begins with those?

Nine new neckties
and a nightshirt
and a nose.

O is very useful.
You use it when you say:
"Oscar's only ostrich
oiled
an orange owl today."

# ABCD
# EFG
# HIJK
# LMNO..

...P

Painting pink pyjamas.
Policeman in a pail.

Peter Pepper's puppy.
And now
Papa's in the pail.

# BIG Q

little q

What begins with Q ?

The quick
Queen of Quincy
and her
quacking quacker-oo.

QUACK
QUACK

41

# BIG R
## little r
## Rosy Robin Ross.

Rosy's going riding
on her
red rhinoceros.

# BIG S

little      s

Silly Sammy Slick
sipped six sodas
and got
sick sick sick.

45

# T....T

## t.......t

What begins with T?

Ten tired turtles
on a tuttle-tuttle tree.

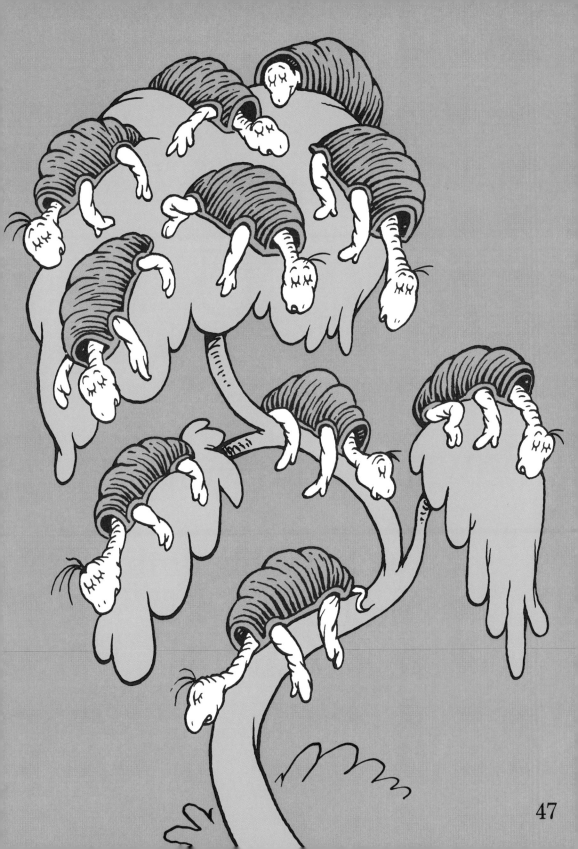

# BIG U

little          u

What begins with U?

Uncle Ubb's umbrella
and his
underwear, too.

# BIG V

little      v

Vera Violet Vinn
 is
very
very
very awful
on her violin.

W . . w . . W

Willy Waterloo
washes Warren Wiggins
who is
washing Waldo Woo.

X is very useful
if your name is
Nixie Knox.
It also
comes in handy
spelling axe
and extra fox.

NIXIE KNOX

# BIG Y
## little y

A yawning yellow yak.
Young Yolanda Yorgenson
is yelling on his back.

QRS
TUV...

W..X
Y.. and ....

# BIG Z

little        z

What begins with Z?

I do.

I am a
Zizzer-Zazzer-Zuzz
as you can
plainly see.